D1602173

60 Handel Overtures

Arranged for Solo Keyboard

GEORGE FRIDERIC HANDEL

DOVER PUBLICATIONS, INC.
New York

Published in Canada by General Publishing Company, Ltd., 30 Lesmill Road, Don Mills, Toronto, Ontario.
Published in the United Kingdom by Constable and Company, Ltd., 3 The Lanchesters, 162–164 Fulham Palace Road, London W6 9ER.

Bibliographical Note

This Dover edition, first published in 1993, is a republication of *Handel's Sixty Overtures from all his Operas and Oratorios Set for the Harpsicord or Organ*, originally published by John Walsh, London, n.d. (but prior to 1756). With the exception of minor corrections to improve legibility, the musical text is unabridged and unaltered. The Publisher's Note, Contents and Alphabetical List of Overtures have been specially prepared for this edition.

The publisher wishes to thank the Hutterian Society of Norfolk, Connecticut, for loaning the original volume for reproduction, and Carl Dudash for arranging the loan.

Library of Congress Cataloging-in-Publication Data

Handel, George Frideric, 1685–1759.
    [Overtures. Selections; arr]
    60 Handel overtures arranged for solo keyboard / George Frideric Handel.
        p.   cm.
    Reprint. Originally published: Handel's sixty overtures from all his operas and oratorios set for the harpsicord or organ. London : J. Walsh, ca. 1755.
    ISBN 0-486-27744-5
    1. Overtures (Keyboard instrument), Arranged.   I. Title.   II. Title: Sixty Handel overtures arranged for solo keyboard.
M35.H   93-23949
                                                                                                                  CIP
                                                                                                                    M

Manufactured in the United States of America
Dover Publications, Inc., 31 East 2nd Street, Mineola, N.Y. 11501

Publisher's Note

T HE SIXTY WORKS presented here in arrangements for solo keyboard, as originally published by Handel's London publisher John Walsh (the younger), are drawn from secular and sacred dramatic works from 1708 to approximately 1750; that is, from the earliest of the Italian operas to the full flowering of the oratorios in English. The arrangements are accurate transcriptions of their orchestral counterparts, retaining the contrapuntal textures of the fugal allegro sections and capturing the grandeur of the slow introductions; yet they possess an authentic keyboard quality that sets them apart from the usual hack arrangement, common in Handel's day and plaguing musicians ever since. The arrangements are ornamented in the manner of the day; see below for a further discussion of this topic.

With the growing interest in Handel's Italian stage works, the original Italian names of the operas may be more familiar than the anglicized versions used in Walsh's publication. For the most part the correspondence is obvious and will not lead to confusion, but for convenience all the Italian equivalents have been added to the alphabetical list of overtures in the present volume. Although most of the works are correctly identified as overtures, some, the so-called "Second Overtures," are more accurately sinfonias or preludes to subsequent acts. The most famous of these "Second Overtures" is that of *Solomon*, commonly known as "The Arrival of the Queen of Sheba."

The title of the original Walsh edition reads: "HANDEL'S SIXTY OVERTURES from all his OPERAS and ORATORIOS set for the HARPSICORD or ORGAN." Although the edition bears no date of publication, it is possible to infer one by examining the contents. Indeed, "all" of Handel's overtures are not included: the many pastiches, cobbled together for specific occasions, are ignored completely. More importantly, the overtures to *Theodora*, *The Choice of Hercules*, *Jephtha* and *The Triumph of Time and Truth* are missing. *Theodora* appeared in 1750, while *Solomon*, the latest in time of the dramatic works presented here, was first given in 1749. If we assume that John Walsh's intention in publishing these arrangements was to capitalize on the popularity of Handel's most recent successes, we can safely ascribe a publication date of 1749–50.* The identity of the arranger is a mystery, although the vogue for keyboard arrangements of Handel's works had existed since the 1720s, owing largely to the wide circulation of bravura arrangements and variations based on arias from the Italian operas made by the English harpsichordist William Babell.

With the exception of two very short passages, which have been tacitly reconstructed where the original was illegible, the music has been reprinted exactly as it appears in the original Walsh edition. The typographical errors are few, generally insignificant, and obvious to the alert musician. The performer's attention is drawn to certain characteristics of the typography which may be unfamiliar. The value-dot, rather than being placed next to the note whose value the dot increases, as in modern notation, is placed at the point in the musical text corresponding to the added value which the dot represents, thus: . The principle holds, even across bar lines, thus:

---

*The volume is certainly no later than 1756, the date an owner inscribed on the copy reproduced here.

In a few places, this copy also contains music notes handwritten by an early owner, added to complete a harmony or thicken the texture.

Quarter-note rests appear as simple right-angles ($\ulcorner$). The ornaments are standard, the trill sign being represented uniformly by the symbol tr . The mordent is shown in a variety of forms, (m , $+$, $\sim\!\!\!\!\sim$) but the variations seem to be due to the various engravers' individual styles, rather than to any intended variation in the execution of the ornament. In fact, the ornamentation may be largely arbitrary: an examination of the Chrysander edition of the full scores, based on original performance materials and the different extant versions of the original scores, shows many discrepancies between what may justifiably be considered Handel's own intentions and these keyboard arrangements. At any rate, the issue of ornamentation was generally left to the discretion and musical taste of the performer and the same holds true to the present.

Perhaps the most jarring convention is the occasional appearance in the left hand of passages written in the tenor C-clef. This would seem to result from the direct adoption of the solo cello line of the full score and has the typographical benefit of avoiding the use of more than one ledger-line. The C-clef is so named because the position of its middle point on the staff denotes the placement of middle C. This information will assist the clef-impaired performer in calculating the progression of his left hand.

Contents

	Page
Overture in Parthenope	1
Overture in Lotharius	5
Overture in Ptolomy [Ptolemy]	10
Overture in Siroe	14
Overture in Richard the 1st	18
Overture in Admetus	21
Second Overture in Admetus	24
Overture in Alexander	27
Overture in Scipio	31
Overture in Rodelinda	35
Overture in Tamerlane	38
Second Overture in Amadis	42
Overture in Julius Caesar	45
Overture in Flavius	50
Overture in Acis and Galatea	53
Overture in Radamistus	57
Overture in Amadis	60
Overture in the Water Musick	64
Overture in Theseus	67
Overture in Pastor Fido	73
Overture in Otho	82
Overture in Muzio Scevola	86
Overture in Floridant	88
The Overture of Rinaldo	91
Overture in Ariadne	95
Overture in Orlando	100
Overture in Sosarmes	104
Overture in Ætius	108
Overture in Porus	110
Overture in Esther	113
Overture in Justin	119

	Page
Overture in Arminius	125
Overture in Atalanta	129
Overture in Alcina	134
Overture in Ariodante	138
Second Overture in Pastor Fido	143
Overture in Xerxes	148
Overture in Alexander's Feast	153
Overture in Faramondo	156
Overture in Berenice	160
Overture in Alexander Severus	164
Overture in Athalia	169
Overture in Messiah	173
Overture in Samson	176
Overture in Saul	181
Overture in Deidamia	189
Overture in Hymen	193
Overture in Parnasso in Festa	197
Overture in the Occasional Oratorio	202
Overture in Belshazzar	208
Overture in Joseph	211
Overture in Hercules	216
Overture in Semele	221
Second Overture in Saul	226
Overture in Solomon	229
Overture in Susanna	234
Overture in Alexander Balus	238
Overture in Joshua	241
Overture in Judas Maccabaeus	246
Second Overture in Solomon (Sinfonia, *The Arrival of the Queen of Sheba*)	251

List of Overtures
in Alphabetical Order

	Page		*Page*
Acis and Galatea	53	Lotharius (Lotario)	5
Admetus (Admeto, Rè di Tessaglia)	21	Messiah	173
Admetus, Second Overture	24	Muzio Scevola	86
Ætius (Ezio)	108	Occasional Oratorio	202
Alcina	134	Orlando	100
Alexander (Alessandro)	27	Otho (Ottone, Rè di Germania)	82
Alexander Balus	238	Parnasso in Festa, Il	197
Alexander Severus (Alessandro Severo)	164	Parthenope (Partenope)	1
Alexander's Feast	153	Pastor Fido, Il	73
Amadis (Amadigi di Gaula)	60	Pastor Fido, Il, Second Overture	143
Amadis, Second Overture	42	Porus (Poro, Rè dell'Indie)	110
Ariadne (Arianna in Creta)	95	Ptolomy [Ptolemy] (Tolomeo, Rè di Egitto)	10
Ariodante	138	Radamistus (Radamisto)	57
Arminius (Arminio)	125	Richard the 1st (Riccardo Primo, Rè d'Inghilterra)	18
Arrival of the Queen of Sheba	251	Rinaldo	91
Atalanta	129	Rodelinda (Rodelinda, Regina de'Longobardi)	35
Athalia	169	Samson	176
Belshazzar	208	Saul	181
Berenice	160	Saul, Second Overture	226
Deidamia	189	Scipio (Scipione)	31
Esther	113	Semele	221
Faramondo	156	Siroe (Siroe, Rè di Persia)	14
Flavius (Flavio, Rè di Longobardi)	50	Solomon	229
Floridant (Floridante)	88	Solomon, Second Overture	251
Hercules	216	Sosarmes	104
Hymen (Imeneo)	193	Susanna	234
Joseph [and His Brethren]	211	Tamerlane (Tamerlano)	38
Joshua	241	Theseus (Teseo)	67
Judas Maccabaeus	246	Water Musick	64
Julius Caesar (Giulio Cesare in Egitto)	45	Xerxes (Serse)	148
Justin (Giustino)	119		

HANDEL'S sixty OVERTURES
from all his OPERAS and ORATORIOS
Set for the
HARPSICORD or ORGAN.
viz.

	N.º		N.º		N.º
ADMETUS	VI	FLAVIUS	XIV	PHARAMOND	XXXIX
ADMETUS 2d	VII	FLORIDANT	XXIII	PERNASSO IN FESTA	XLVIII
ALEXANDER	VIII	HYMEN	XLVII	RICHARD the 1st	V
AMADIS	XII	HERCULES	LII	RODELINDA	X
ACIS & GALATEA	XV	JULIUS CÆSAR	XIII	RADAMISTUS	XVI
AMADIS 2d	YVII	JUSTIN	XXXI	RINALDO	XXIV
ARIADNE	XXV	JOSEPH	LI	SIROE	IV
ÆTIUS	XXVIII	JOSHUA	LVIII	SCIPIO	IX
ARMINIUS	XXXII	JUDAS MACCABEUS	LIX	SOSARMES	XXVII
ATALANTA	XXXIII	LOTHARIUS	II	SAMSON	XLIV
ALCINA	XXXIV	MUZIO SCÆVOLA	XXII	SAUL	XLV
ARIODANTE	XXXV	MESSIAH	XLIII	SEMELE	LIII
ALEXANDER'S FEAST	XXXVIII	OTHO	XXI	SAUL 2d	LIV
ALEXANDER SEVERUS	XLI	ORLANDO	XXVI	SOLOMON	LV
ATHALIA	XLII	OCCASIONAL Oratorio	XLIX	SUSANNA	LVI
ALEXANDER BALUS	LVII	PARTHENOPE	I	SOLOMON 2d	LX
BERENICE	XL	PTOLOMY	III	TAMERLANE	XI
BELSHAZZAR	L	PASTOR FIDO	XX	THESEUS	XIX
DEIDAMIA	XLVI	PORUS	XXIX	WATER MUSICK	XVIII
ESTHER	XXX	PASTOR FIDO 2d	XXXVI	XERXES	XXXVII

N.B. The above Overtures may be had for Concerts for Violins in 8 Parts.

London. *Printed for* I. Walsh *in Catharine Street in y̆ Strand.*

Of whom may be had for the Harpsicord or Organ

Handel's 240 Songs Selected from his Oratorios, in 3 Volumes.	St Martini's Concertos
Fire and Water Musick	Rameau's Concertos
2 Volumes of Lessons	Stanley's Concertos
6 Fugues or Voluntaries	Avison's Concertos
12 Organ Concertos	Mondonville's Lessons
Collection of Dance Tunes	Ciampi's Lessons
12 Solos	Alberti's Lessons
Aires from all his Operas and Oratorios, in 6 Volumes	Burney's Cornet Pieces
Operas and Oratorios in Score	Pescetti's Lessons

ORIGINAL TITLE PAGE

60 Handel Overtures

Overture in Parthenope

Volti

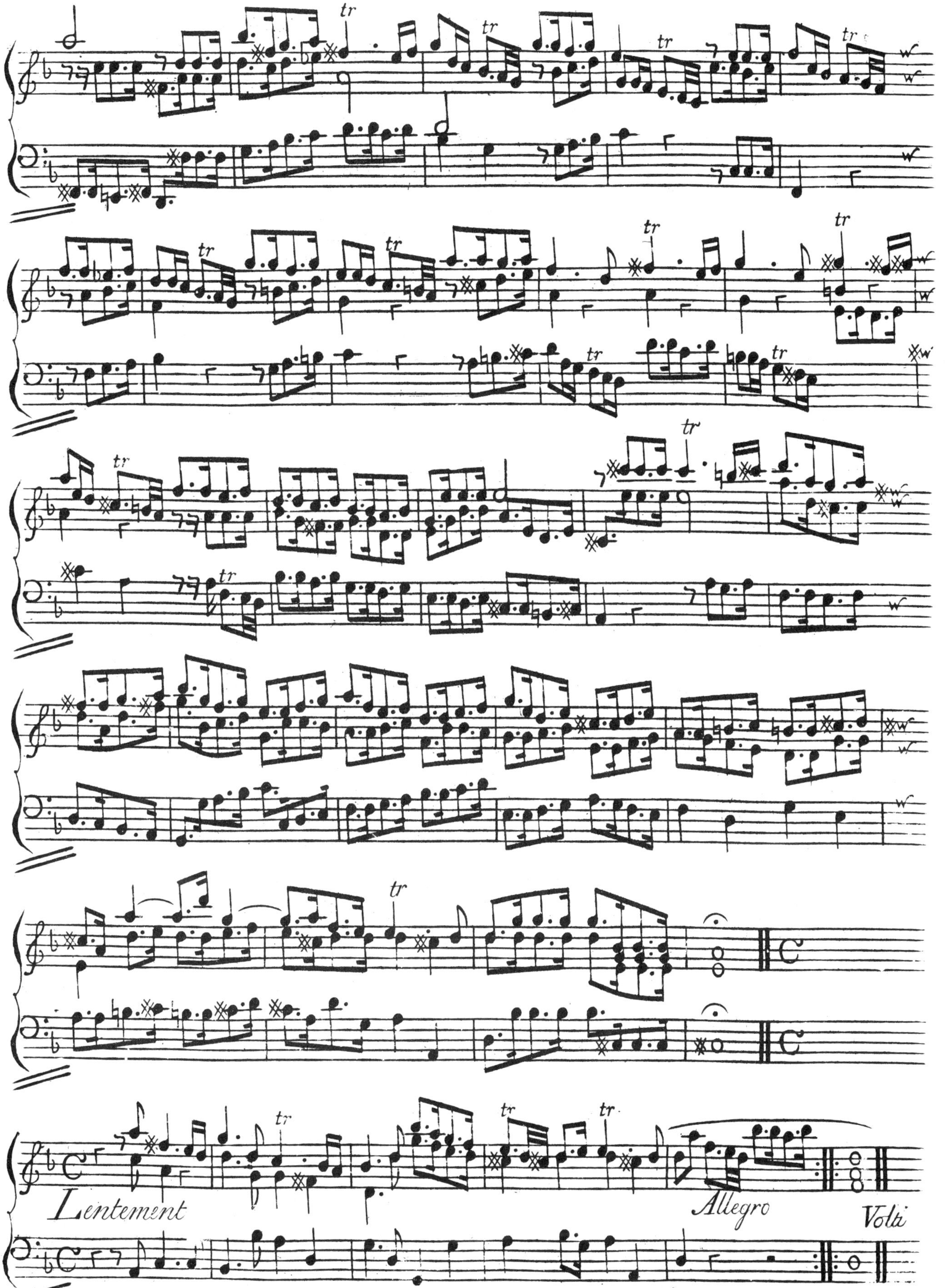
Lentement
Allegro
Volti

Overture in Lotharius

Volti

Volti

Overture in Ptolomy [Ptolemy]

Volti

Volti

Overture in Siroe

Volti

Volti

Overture in Richard the 1st

Volti

Allegro

Overture in Admetus

Volti

Second Overture in Admetus

Volti

Overture in Alexander

Overture in Scipio

Overture in Rodelinda

Overture in Tamerlane

Menuet

Second Overture in Amadis

Volti

Finis

Overture in Julius Caesar

Overture in Flavius

Overture in Acis and Galatea

Volti

Overture in Radamistus

Overture in Amadis

Overture in the Water Musick

Overture in Theseus

Finis

Overture in Pastor Fido

Volti

Volti

Overture in Otho

GAVOTTA

Overture in Muzio Scevola

Overture in Floridant

The Overture of Rinaldo

Volti

Da Capo al Segno

Adagio

Giga Presto

Fine

Overture in Ariadne

Allegro

Overture in Orlando

Lentement

Gigue Allegro

Overture in Sosarmes

Allegro

106   *Sosarmes*

Overture in Ætius

Overture in Porus

Allegro

Overture in Esther

Andante

Volti Subito

Larghetto

Volti Subito

Overture in Justin

Volti Subito

120
Justin

Overture in Arminius

Volti Subito

Overture in Atalanta

Volti

Allegro

130   *Atalanta*

Volti Subito

Overture in Alcina

Volti Subito

Alcina   135

Overture in Ariodante

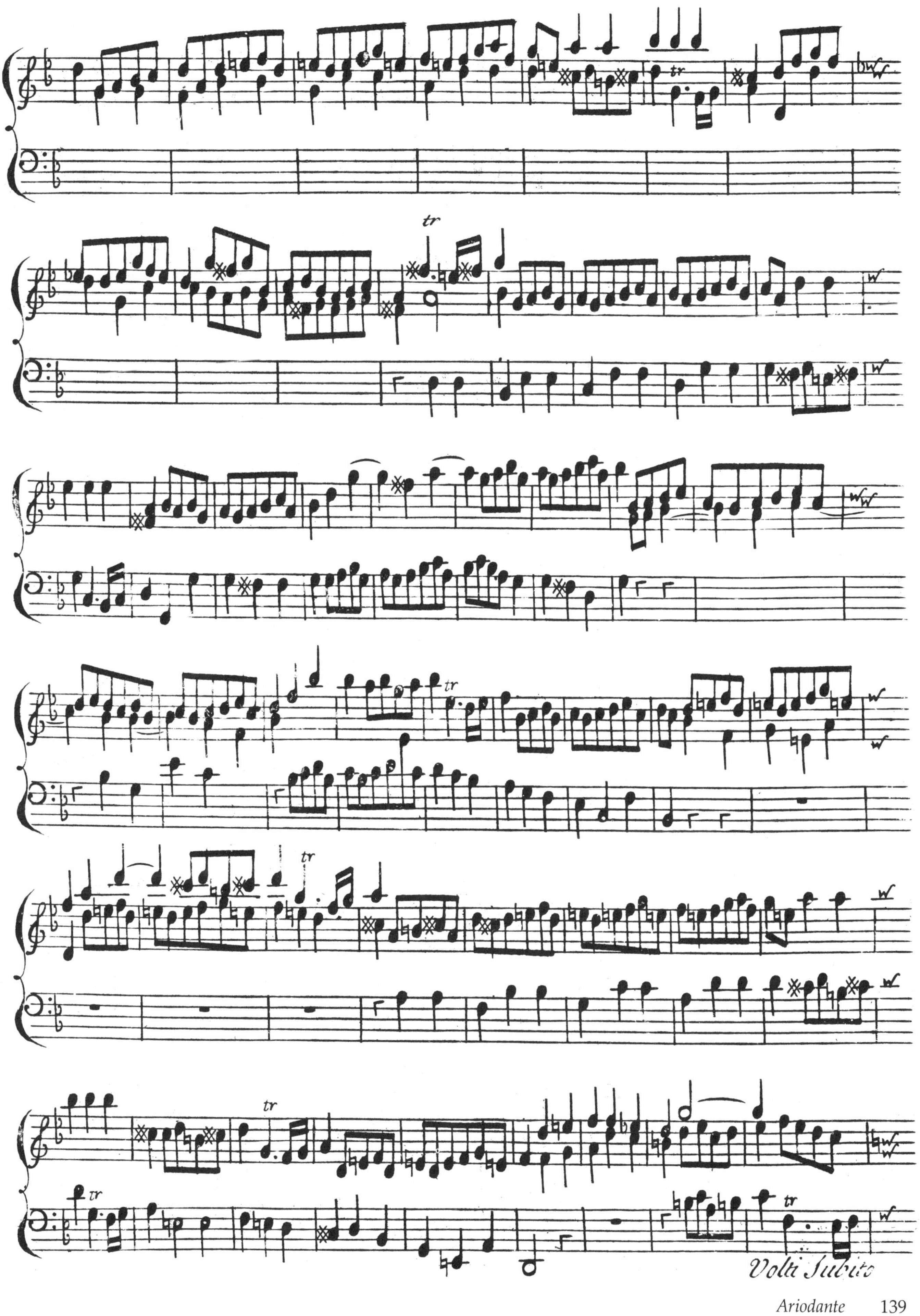
tr
Volti Subito

Ariodante 141

142   *Ariodante*

Second Overture in Pastor Fido

Allegro

Volti Subito

2nd Pastor Fido   145

A tempo di Bouree

Overture in Xerxes

Volti

Volti

Gigue

Overture in Alexander's Feast

154   *Alexander's Feast*

Overture in Faramondo

Overture in Berenice

Andante Larghetto

Volti

162   *Berenice*

Overture in Alexander Severus

Allegro   *Volti*

Allegro

Overture in Athalia

Overture in Messiah

Overture in Samson

Adagio

Da Capo al Segno :S:

Overture in Saul

182   *Saul*

Overture in Deidamia

Overture in Hymen

Overture in Parnasso in Festa

Overture in the Occasional Oratorio

March

Overture in Belshazzar

Overture in Joseph

Overture in Hercules

Minuet

Overture in Semele

Second Overture in Saul

Overture in Solomon

Allegro Moderato

Overture in Susanna

Non troppo Allegro

Lentement

Overture in Alexander Balus

Overture in Joshua

A Tempo Ordinario

A Tempo Ordinario

Overture in Judas Maccabaeus

March in Judas Maccabus

Second Overture in Solomon
(Sinfonia, *The Arrival of the Queen of Sheba*)

254   *2nd Solomon*

Dover Piano and Keyboard Editions

THE WELL-TEMPERED CLAVIER: Books I and II, Complete, Johann Sebastian Bach. All 48 preludes and fugues in all major and minor keys. Authoritative Bach-Gesellschaft edition. Explanation of ornaments in English, tempo indications, music corrections. 208pp. 9⅜ × 12¼. 24532-2 Pa. **$9.95**

KEYBOARD MUSIC, J. S. Bach. Bach-Gesellschaft edition. For harpsichord, piano, other keyboard instruments. English Suites, French Suites, Six Partitas, Goldberg Variations, Two-Part Inventions, Three-Part Sinfonias. 312pp. 8⅛ × 11. 22360-4 Pa. **$11.95**

ITALIAN CONCERTO, CHROMATIC FANTASIA AND FUGUE AND OTHER WORKS FOR KEYBOARD, Johann Sebastian Bach. Sixteen of Bach's best-known, most-performed and most-recorded works for the keyboard, reproduced from the authoritative Bach-Gesellschaft edition. 112pp. 9 × 12. 25387-2 Pa. **$8.95**

COMPLETE KEYBOARD TRANSCRIPTIONS OF CONCERTOS BY BAROQUE COMPOSERS, Johann Sebastian Bach. Sixteen concertos by Vivaldi, Telemann and others, transcribed for solo keyboard instruments. Bach-Gesellschaft edition. 128pp. 9⅜ × 12¼. 25529-8 Pa. **$8.95**

ORGAN MUSIC, J. S. Bach. Bach-Gesellschaft edition. 93 works. 6 Trio Sonatas, German Organ Mass, Orgelbüchlein, Six Schubler Chorales, 18 Choral Preludes. 357pp. 8⅛ × 11. 22359-0 Pa. **$12.95**

COMPLETE PRELUDES AND FUGUES FOR ORGAN, Johann Sebastian Bach. All 25 of Bach's complete sets of preludes and fugues (i.e. compositions written as pairs), from the authoritative Bach-Gesellschaft edition. 168pp. 8⅜ × 11. 24816-X Pa. **$9.95**

TOCCATAS, FANTASIAS, PASSACAGLIA AND OTHER WORKS FOR ORGAN, J. S. Bach. Over 20 best-loved works including Toccata and Fugue in D minor, BWV 565; Passacaglia and Fugue in C minor, BWV 582, many more. Bach-Gesellschaft edition. 176pp. 9 × 12. 25403-8 Pa. **$9.95**

TWO- AND THREE-PART INVENTIONS, J. S. Bach. Reproduction of original autograph ms. Edited by Eric Simon. 62pp. 8⅛ × 11. 21982-8 Pa. **$8.95**

THE 36 FANTASIAS FOR KEYBOARD, Georg Philipp Telemann. Graceful compositions by 18th-century master. 1923 Breslauer edition. 80pp. 8⅛ × 11. 25365-1 Pa. **$5.95**

GREAT KEYBOARD SONATAS, Carl Philipp Emanuel Bach. Comprehensive two-volume edition contains 51 sonatas by second, most important son of Johann Sebastian Bach. Originality, rich harmony, delicate workmanship. Authoritative French edition. Total of 384pp. 8⅜ × 11¼. Series I 24853-4 Pa. **$9.95** Series II 24854-2 Pa. **$10.95**

KEYBOARD WORKS/Series One: Ordres I–XIII; Series Two: Ordres XIV–XXVII and Miscellaneous Pieces, François Couperin. Over 200 pieces. Reproduced directly from edition prepared by Johannes Brahms and Friedrich Chrysander. Total of 496pp. 8⅛ × 11. Series I 25795-9 Pa. **$10.95** Series II 25796-7 Pa. **$11.95**

KEYBOARD WORKS FOR SOLO INSTRUMENTS, G. F. Handel. 35 neglected works from Handel's vast oeuvre, originally jotted down as improvisations. Includes Eight Great Suites, others. New sequence. 174pp. 9⅜ × 12¼. 24338-9 Pa. **$9.95**

WORKS FOR ORGAN AND KEYBOARD, Jan Pieterszoon Sweelinck. Nearly all of early Dutch composer's difficult-to-find keyboard works. Chorale variations; toccatas, fantasias; variations on secular, dance tunes. Also, incomplete and/or modified works, plus fantasia by John Bull. 272pp. 9 × 12. 24935-2 Pa. **$12.95**

ORGAN WORKS, Dietrich Buxtehude. Complete organ works o extremely influential pre-Bach composer. Toccatas, preludes, chorales more. Definitive Breitkopf & Härtel edition. 320pp. 8⅜ × 11¼. (Availabl in U.S. only) 25682-0 Pa. **$12.9**

THE FUGUES ON THE MAGNIFICAT FOR ORGAN OR KEY BOARD, Johann Pachelbel. 94 pieces representative of Pachelbel' magnificent contribution to keyboard composition; can be played or the organ, harpsichord or piano. 100pp. 9 × 12. (Available in U.S only) 25037-7 Pa. **$7.9**

MY LADY NEVELLS BOOKE OF VIRGINAL MUSIC, William Byrd. 42 compositions in modern notation from 1591 ms. For an keyboard instrument. 245pp. 8⅛ × 11. 22246-2 Pa. **$13.9**

ELIZABETH ROGERS HIR VIRGINALL BOOKE, edited wit calligraphy by Charles J. F. Cofone. All 112 pieces from noted 165 manuscript, most never before published. Composers include Thoma Brewer, William Byrd, Orlando Gibbons, etc. 125pp. 9 × 12. 23138-0 Pa. **$10.**

THE FITZWILLIAM VIRGINAL BOOK, edited by J. Fuller Mait land, W. B. Squire. Famous early 17th-century collection of keyboar music, 300 works by Morley, Byrd, Bull, Gibbons, etc. Moder notation. Total of 938pp. 8⅜ × 11. Two-vol. set. 21068-5, 21069-3 Pa. **$33.9**

GREAT KEYBOARD SONATAS, Series I and Series II, Domenic Scarlatti. 78 of the most popular sonatas reproduced from the G Ricordi edition edited by Alessandro Longo. Total of 320pp. 8⅜ × 11¼ Series I 24996-4 Pa. **$8.9** Series II 25003-2 Pa. **$8.9**

SONATAS AND FANTASIES FOR THE PIANO, W. A. Mozar edited by Nathan Broder. Finest, most accurate edition, based o autographs and earliest editions. 19 sonatas, plus Fantasy and Fugue i C, K.394, Fantasy in C Minor, K.396, Fantasy in D Minor, K.397. 352pp 9 × 12. (Available in U.S. only) 25417-8 Pa. **$16.5**

COMPLETE PIANO SONATAS, Joseph Haydn. 52 sonatas reprinte from authoritative Breitkopf & Härtel edition. Extremely clear an readable; ample space for notes, analysis. 464pp. 9⅜ × 12¼. 24726-0 Pa. **$10.9** 24727-9 Pa. **$11.9**

BAGATELLES, RONDOS AND OTHER SHORTER WORKS FO PIANO, Ludwig van Beethoven. Most popular and most performe shorter works, including Rondo a capriccio in G and Andante in F Breitkopf & Härtel edition. 128pp. 9⅜ × 12¼. 25392-9 Pa. **$8.9**

COMPLETE VARIATIONS FOR SOLO PIANO, Ludwig va Beethoven. Contains all 21 sets of Beethoven's piano variations including the extremely popular *Diabelli Variations, Op. 120.* 240pp 9⅜ × 12¼. 25188-8 Pa. **$11.9**

COMPLETE PIANO SONATAS, Ludwig van Beethoven. All sonata in fine Schenker edition, with fingering, analytical material. One o best modern editions. 615pp. 9 × 12. Two-vol. set. 23134-8, 23135-6 Pa. **$25.9**

COMPLETE SONATAS FOR PIANOFORTE SOLO, Fran Schubert. All 15 sonatas. Breitkopf and Härtel edition. 293pp. 9⅜ × 12¼ 22647-6 Pa. **$13.9**

DANCES FOR SOLO PIANO, Franz Schubert. Over 350 waltzes minuets, landler, ecossaises, other charming, melodic dance compositions reprinted from the authoritative Breitkopf & Härtel edition. 192pp. 9⅜ × 12¼. 26107-7 Pa. **$10.95**

*Available from your music dealer or write for **free** Music Catalog to Dover Publications, Inc., Dept. MUBI, 31 East 2nd Street, Mineola, N.Y. 11501.*

Dover Piano and Keyboard Editions

ORGAN WORKS, César Franck. Composer's best-known works for organ, including Six Pieces, Trois Pieces, and Trois Chorals. Oblong format for easy use at keyboard. Authoritative Durand edition. 208pp. 11⅜ × 8¼. 25517-4 Pa. **$12.95**

IBERIA AND ESPAÑA: Two Complete Works for Solo Piano, Isaac Albeniz. Spanish composer's greatest piano works in authoritative editions. Includes the popular "Tango". 192pp. 9 × 12. 25367-8 Pa. **$10.95**

GOYESCAS, SPANISH DANCES AND OTHER WORKS FOR SOLO PIANO, Enrique Granados. Great Spanish composer's most admired, most performed suites for the piano, in definitive Spanish editions. 176pp. 9 × 12. 25481-X Pa. **$8.95**

SELECTED PIANO COMPOSITIONS, César Franck, edited by Vincent d'Indy. Outstanding selection of influential French composer's piano works, including early pieces and the two masterpieces—Prelude, Choral and Fugue; and Prelude, Aria and Finale. Ten works in all. 138pp. 9 × 12. 23269-7 Pa. **$10.95**

THE COMPLETE PRELUDES AND ETUDES FOR PIANOFORTE SOLO, Alexander Scriabin. All the preludes and études including many perfectly spun miniatures. Edited by K. N. Igumnov and Y. I. Mil'shteyn. 250pp. 9 × 12. 22919-X Pa. **$10.95**

COMPLETE PIANO SONATAS, Alexander Scriabin. All ten of Scriabin's sonatas, reprinted from an authoritative early Russian edition. 256pp. 8⅜ × 11¼. 25850-5 Pa. **$11.95**

COMPLETE PRELUDES AND ETUDES-TABLEAUX, Serge Rachmaninoff. Forty-one of his greatest works for solo piano, including the riveting C minor, G-minor and B-minor preludes, in authoritative editions. 208pp. 8⅜ × 11¼. 25696-0 Pa. **$10.95**

COMPLETE PIANO SONATAS, Sergei Prokofiev. Definitive Russian edition of nine sonatas (1907–1953), among the most important compositions in the modern piano repertoire. 288pp. 8⅜ × 11¼. (Available in U.S. only) 25689-8 Pa. **$11.95**

GYMNOPÉDIES, GNOSSIENNES AND OTHER WORKS FOR PIANO, Erik Satie. The largest Satie collection of piano works yet published, 17 in all, reprinted from the original French editions. 176pp. 9 × 12. (Not available in France or Germany) 25978-1 Pa. **$9.95**

TWENTY SHORT PIECES FOR PIANO (Sports et Divertissements), Erik Satie. French master's brilliant thumbnail sketches—verbal and musical—of various outdoor sports and amusements. English translations, 20 illustrations. Rare, limited 1925 edition. 48pp. 12 × 8⅞. (Not available in France or Germany) 24365-6 Pa. **$5.95**

COMPLETE PRELUDES, IMPROMPTUS AND VALSES-CA-PRICES, Gabriel Fauré. Eighteen elegantly wrought piano works in authoritative editions. Only one-volume collection. 144pp. 9 × 12. (Not available in France or Germany) 25789-4 Pa. **$8.95**

PIANO MUSIC OF BÉLA BARTÓK, Series I, Béla Bartók. New, definitive Archive Edition incorporating composer's corrections. Includes *Funeral March* from *Kossuth, Fourteen Bagatelles,* Bartók's break to modernism. 167pp. 9 × 12. (Available in U.S. only) 24108-4 Pa. **$10.95**

PIANO MUSIC OF BÉLA BARTÓK, Series II, Béla Bartók. Second in the Archie Edition incorporating composer's corrections. 85 short pieces *For Children, Two Elegies, Two Rumanian Dances,* etc. 192pp. 9 × 12. (Available in U.S. only) 24109-2 Pa. **$10.95**

FRENCH PIANO MUSIC, AN ANTHOLOGY, Isidor Phillipp (ed.). 44 complete works, 1670–1905, by Lully, Couperin, Rameau, Alkan, Saint-Saëns, Delibes, Bizet, Godard, many others; favorites, lesser-known examples, but all top quality. 188pp. 9 × 12. (Not available in France or Germany) 23381-2 Pa. **$9.95**

NINETEENTH-CENTURY EUROPEAN PIANO MUSIC: Unfamiliar Masterworks, John Gillespie (ed.). Difficult-to-find études, toccatas, polkas, impromptus, waltzes, etc., by Albéniz, Bizet, Chabrier, Fauré, Smetana, Richard Strauss, Wagner and 16 other composers. 62 pieces. 343pp. 9 × 12. (Not available in France or Germany) 23447-9 Pa. **$15.95**

RARE MASTERPIECES OF RUSSIAN PIANO MUSIC: Eleven Pieces by Glinka, Balakirev, Glazunov and Others, edited by Dmitry Feofanov. Glinka's *Prayer,* Balakirev's *Reverie,* Liapunov's *Transcendental Etude, Op. 11, No. 10,* and eight others—full, authoritative scores from Russian texts. 144pp. 9 × 12. 24659-0 Pa. **$8.95**

HUMORESQUES AND OTHER WORKS FOR SOLO PIANO, Antonin Dvořák. Humoresques, Op. 101, complete, Silhouettes, Op. 8, Poetic Tone Pictures, Theme with Variations, Op. 36, 4 Slavonic Dances, more. 160pp. 9 × 12. 28355-0 Pa. **$9.95**

PIANO MUSIC, Louis M. Gottschalk. 26 pieces (including covers) by early 19th-century American genius. "Bamboula," "The Banjo," other Creole, Negro-based material, through elegant salon music. 301pp. 9¼ × 12. 21683-7 Pa. **$13.95**

SOUSA'S GREAT MARCHES IN PIANO TRANSCRIPTION, John Philip Sousa. Playing edition includes: "The Stars and Stripes Forever," "King Cotton," "Washington Post," much more. 24 illustrations. 111pp. 9 × 12. 23132-1 Pa. **$7.95**

COMPLETE PIANO RAGS, Scott Joplin. All 38 piano rags by the acknowledged master of the form, reprinted from the publisher's original editions complete with sheet music covers. Introduction by David A. Jasen. 208pp. 9 × 12. 25807-6 Pa. **$9.95**

RAGTIME REDISCOVERIES, selected by Trebor Jay Tichenor. 64 unusual rags demonstrate diversity of style, local tradition. Original sheet music. 320pp. 9 × 12. 23776-1 Pa. **$14.95**

RAGTIME RARITIES, edited by Trebor J. Tichenor. 63 tuneful, rediscovered piano rags by 51 composers (or teams). Does not duplicate selections in *Classic Piano Rags* (Dover, 20469-3). 305pp. 9 × 12. 23157-7 Pa. **$12.95**

CLASSIC PIANO RAGS, selected with an introduction by Rudi Blesh. Best ragtime music (1897–1922) by Scott Joplin, James Scott, Joseph F. Lamb, Tom Turpin, nine others. 364pp. 9 × 12. 20469-3 Pa. **$14.95**

RAGTIME GEMS: Original Sheet Music for 25 Ragtime Classics, edited by David A. Jasen. Includes original sheet music and covers for 25 rags, including three of Scott Joplin's finest: *Searchlight Rag, Rose Leaf Rag* and *Fig Leaf Rag.* 122pp. 9 × 12. 25248-5 Pa. **$7.95**

NOCTURNES AND BARCAROLLES FOR SOLO PIANO, Gabriel Fauré. 12 nocturnes and 12 barcarolles reprinted from authoritative French editions. 208pp. 9⅜ × 12¼. (Not available in France or Germany) 27955-3 Pa. **$10.95**

PRELUDES AND FUGUES FOR PIANO, Dmitry Shostakovich. 24 Preludes, Op. 34 and 24 Preludes and Fugues, Op. 87. Reprint of Gosudarstvennoe Izdatel'stvo Muzyka, Moscow, ed. 288pp. 8⅜ × 11. (Available in U.S. only) 26861-6 Pa. **$12.95**

FAVORITE WALTZES, POLKAS AND OTHER DANCES FOR SOLO PIANO, Johann Strauss, Jr. Blue Danube, Tales from Vienna Woods, many other best-known waltzes and other dances. 160pp. 9 × 12. 27851-4 Pa. **$10.95**

SELECTED PIANO WORKS FOR FOUR HANDS, Franz Schubert. 24 separate pieces (16 most popular titles): Three Military Marches, Lebensstürme, Four Polonaises, Four Ländler, etc. Rehearsal numbers added. 273pp. 9 × 12. 23529-7 Pa. **$12.95**

---

*Available from your music dealer or write for **free** Music Catalog to*
Dover Publications, Inc., Dept. MUBI, 31 East 2nd Street, Mineola, N.Y. 11501.